FEARLESS COMPETITORS

MOTOCROSS

GAIL PARMAN

Enslow PUBLISHING

Please visit our website, www.enslow.com. For a free color catalog of all our high-quality books, call toll free 1-800-398-2504 or fax 1-877-980-4454

Published in 2027 by
Enslow Publishing
2544 Clinton Street
Buffalo, NY 14224

Portions of this work were originally authored by Peter Castellano and published as *Daredevil Sports: Motocross*. All new material in this edition is authored by Gail Parman.

Cataloging-in-Publication Data
Names: Parman, Gail.
Title: Motocross / Gail Parman.
Description: Buffalo, NY : Enslow Publishing, 2027. | Series: Fearless competitors | Includes glossary and index.
Identifiers: ISBN 9781978548848 (pbk.) | ISBN 9781978548855 (library bound) | ISBN 9781978548862 (ebook)
Subjects: LCSH: Motocross--Juvenile literature.
Classification: LCC TX811.P377 2027 | DDC 641.34--dc23

Printed in China

Photos Credits: Cover, p. 1, 20 Maciej Kopaniecki/Shutterstock.com; p. 3, 5, 7, 8, 10, 12, 14, 16, 18, 20, 22, 24, 26, 28 (black background) Propakages/Shutterstock.com; p. 3, 24 Eugene Onischenko/Shutterstock.com; p. 4 Cristi Mitu/Shutterstock.com; p. 6 Michalakis Ppalis/Shutterstock.com; p. 7 EchoArt/Shutterstock.com; p. 8, 10 Library of Congress; p. 11 AMA Motorcycle Hall of Fame; p. 12 Dmitry Yashkin/Shutterstock.com; p. 14 OlegRi/Shutterstock.com; p. 16 antoni halim/Shutterstock.com; p. 18 OlegRi/Shutterstock.com; p. 22 Diego Barbieri/Shutterstock.com; p. 28 StepanovA-88/Shutterstock.com; p. 30 Tiden Studio/Shutterstock.com

CPSIA compliance information: Batch #QSENS27: For further information, contact Enslow Publishing, New York, New York, at 1-800-398-2504.

Contents

Dirt Bike Racing 4
The Birth of Motocross 8
Motocross Bikes 12
What to Wear 15
Cross That Finish Line 16
Bring It Inside 22
To the Extreme 24
Freestyle 26
Hop On 28
Safety First 30
For More Information 31
Glossary 32
Index 32

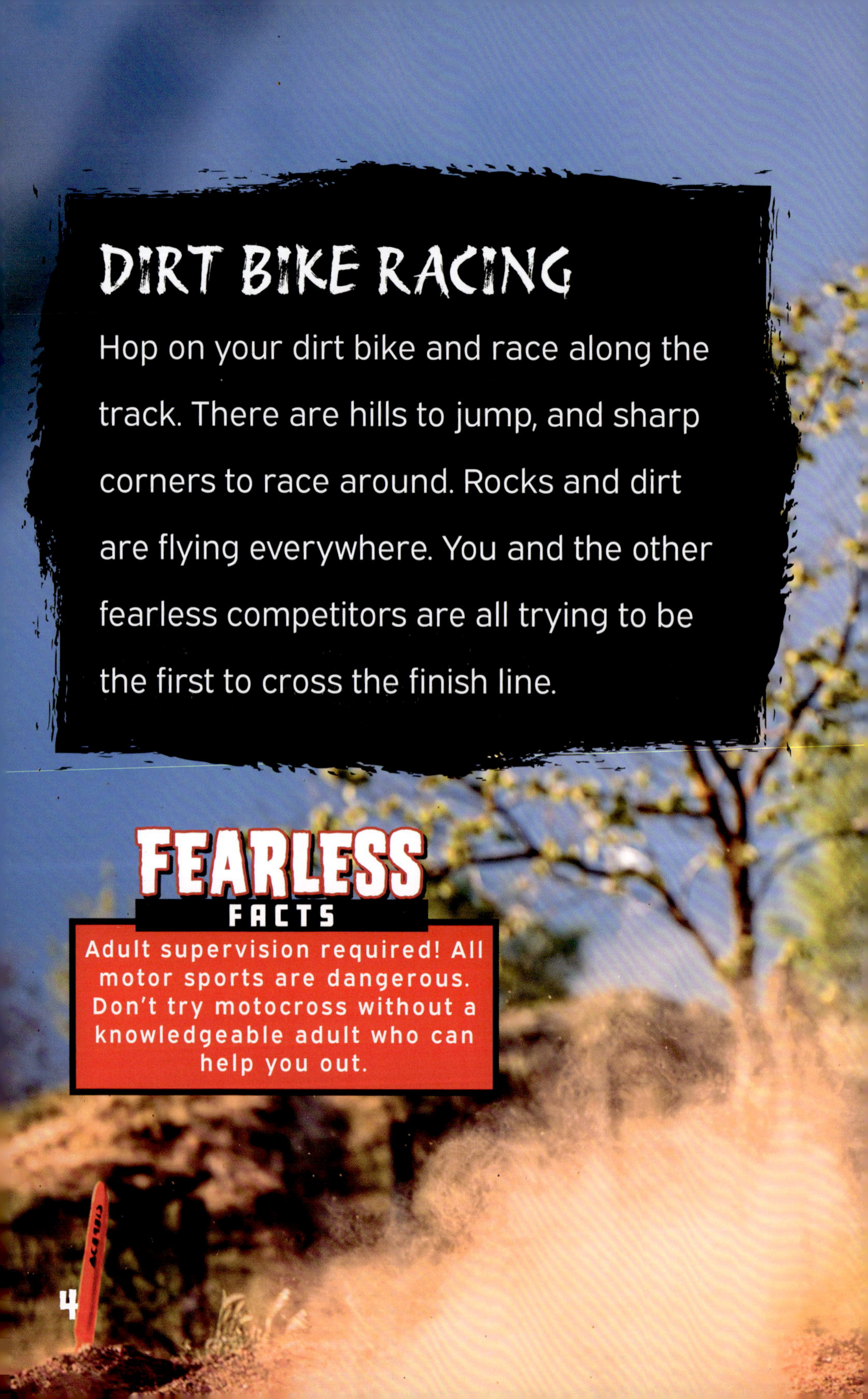

DIRT BIKE RACING

Hop on your dirt bike and race along the track. There are hills to jump, and sharp corners to race around. Rocks and dirt are flying everywhere. You and the other fearless competitors are all trying to be the first to cross the finish line.

FEARLESS FACTS

Adult supervision required! All motor sports are dangerous. Don't try motocross without a knowledgeable adult who can help you out.

411

Motocross is a type of off-road racing sport that involves dirt bikes. It takes place on a dirt track. Racers may face lots of hills and **obstacles**.

FEARLESS FACTS

"Whoops" are common obstacles that involve a series of small rolling hills, one after another. If a rider is going fast enough, they will skip along the tops of the hills!

THE BIRTH OF MOTOCROSS

More than 100 years ago, a club in Great Britain planned a race called the "Southern Scott Scramble." This **event** featured racers speeding around a dirt track. They called the sport "motorcycle scrambling." It would become what we know as motocross today.

FEARLESS FACTS

There were 80 people who started the Southern Scott Scramble, and only 40 finished. The winner finished the 50-mile (80.5-km) race in two hours, one minute, and 51 seconds.

During the 1930s, motorcycle racing grew very popular in Great Britain. After World War II ended, motorcycle scrambling took off in France. The French were the first to call it "motocross," combining "motorcycle" and "cross-country." In the 1960s, motocross made its way to America.

FEARLESS FACTS

Edison Dye is known as the "Father of American Motocross." He brought this style of motorcycle racing from Europe to the United States.

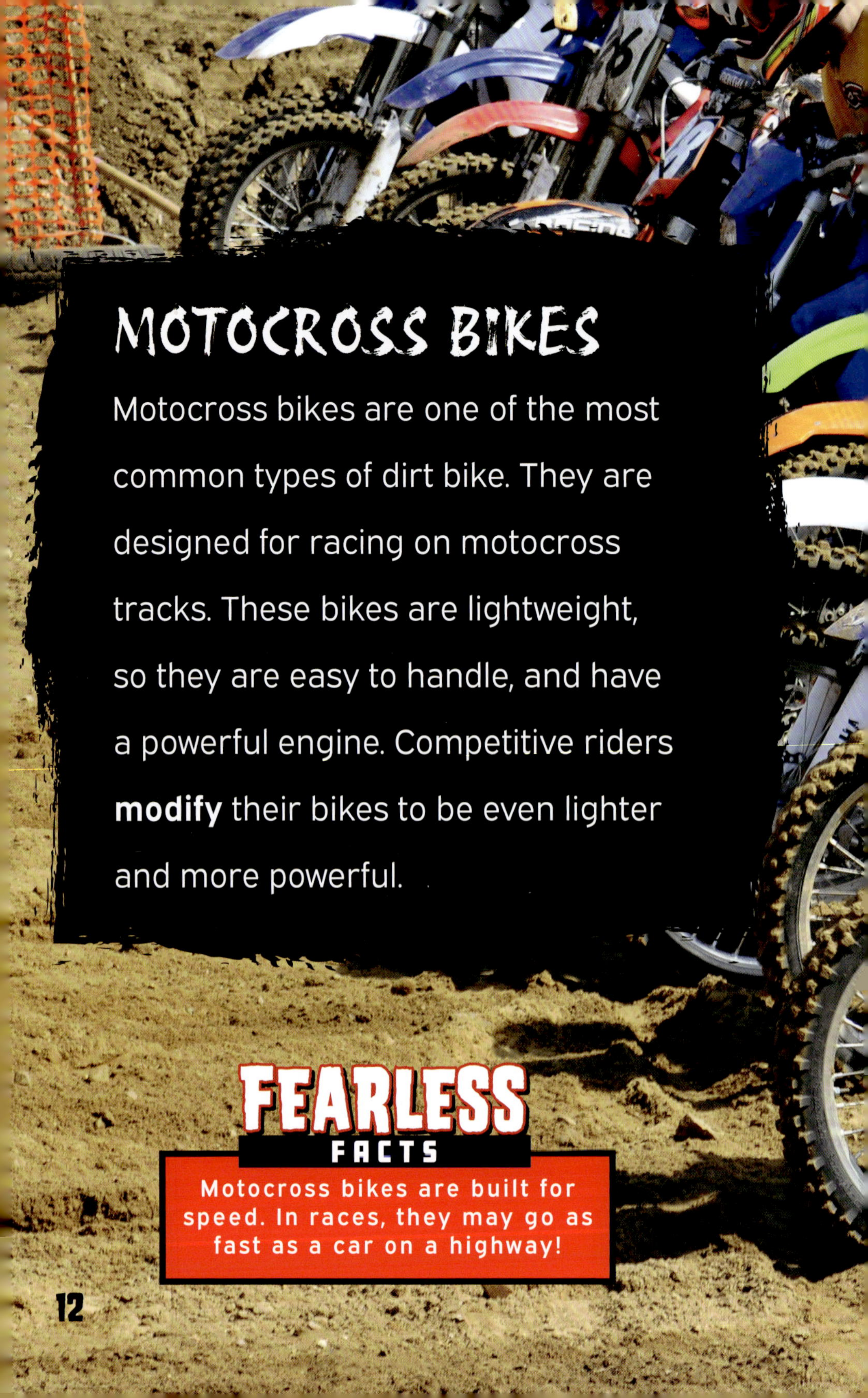

MOTOCROSS BIKES

Motocross bikes are one of the most common types of dirt bike. They are designed for racing on motocross tracks. These bikes are lightweight, so they are easy to handle, and have a powerful engine. Competitive riders **modify** their bikes to be even lighter and more powerful.

FEARLESS FACTS

Motocross bikes are built for speed. In races, they may go as fast as a car on a highway!

SCOTT
Arai
Airoh
SCOTT
SUOMY
CRF
250R
Makita
SUZUKI
BRIDGESTONE
ACERBIS

BĒRZIŅŠ
927
ERIHS
SHOEI
SIDI

WHAT TO WEAR

Motocross riders wear gear that will protect them in case of a crash. A well-fitting helmet with a chin guard is most important. Knee pads are often built in to motocross pants. Riders need boots covering their ankles. They should also wear goggles, gloves, and long-sleeved shirts so they're protected from head to toe. Safety comes first!

FEARLESS FACTS

Everyone falls at some point when racing. After a fall, riders must remember to get themselves and their bike out of the way of other riders. A downed rider on the track could lead to more falls!

CROSS THAT FINISH LINE

Motocross races are usually grouped based on engine size and rider skill level. **Professional** races last 30 minutes plus two laps finished once the race leader reaches the finish line after that time. **Amateur** races are much shorter. These races usually last between eight and 15 minutes.

FEARLESS FACTS

Colored flags are used along race courses to alert riders. Each color has a different meaning. Understanding what each flag means is important for any rider!

The race is under way.

Be careful. There may be an injured rider or a hazard on the track.

The race has been stopped.

Slower riders should be prepared—the leader of the race may be lapping them.

The final lap. This is the last chance for riders to take the lead!

The race is finished.

Most motocross tracks are big enough so that 25 to 30 riders can compete in the same race. The tracks are usually between one and three miles (1.5 and 5 km) long and will include hills, dips, and turns. Before races, riders can walk and ride the track during a practice session. Being aware of the course conditions is important for their safety.

FEARLESS FACTS

Tracks are always changing. New hills or obstacles may be added between races. This keeps the riders on their toes!

LAZER
33
BROCIS
Saldus
288
ALEKSA
Meduspils
O'NEAL
DUNLOP

Motocross is a tough sport, both physically and mentally. Riders use their bodies to control their bikes, so they need to be fit. Some riders compare a motocross event to running very fast for 30 minutes straight! Racers must also stay highly focused in order to make quick decisions.

FEARLESS FACTS

The rules of a motocross race help make sure that riders are being safe and playing fair. Riders who break rules may be **penalized** or even taken out of the race.

BRING IT INSIDE

Supercross is another version of motocross that began in the 1970s. These races take place on a man-made course inside an **arena**, making it easier for people to see all the action. There are lots of tight turns, high jumps, and obstacles. The speedy bikes can usually complete one lap in about 45 to 60 seconds.

FEARLESS FACTS

It takes about 500 truckloads of dirt to build a supercross track.

TO THE EXTREME

Enduro motocross racing combines speed and **endurance**. Imagine a motocross race that lasted three hours and took a rider through creeks, over rocks, and around forests. That's enduro racing. Enduro courses are known for being extremely difficult, so riders need lots of skill and focus.

FEARLESS FACTS

An enduro motocross race in the Republic of Türkiye takes three days to complete. It starts at a beach and ends on top of a mountain!

FREESTYLE

In the 1990s, a new version of motocross was born—freestyle. Freestyle motocross isn't about who's the fastest, but who can do the highest, biggest tricks on their bike. Riders will jump over huge gaps or even spin their bike beneath them! These wild stunts are amazing, but can be extremely dangerous too.

FEARLESS FACTS

The X Games are held every year. The competitions showcase the world's most extreme sports—including freestyle motocross!

ROCKSTAR
ENERGY DRINK
DUNLOP
UVAIRX
IMS

HOP ON

Would you like to try motocross for yourself? First, you need a dirt bike and safety gear. You can take classes to teach you how to ride. And of course, practice, practice, practice! Once you've gotten the hang of riding a dirt bike, you can start picking up speed. The race is on!

FEARLESS FACTS

All riders should check their bike before and after each ride in case there are any problems.

Safety First

ALL MOTOCROSS RIDERS SHOULD:

- wear a helmet, knee pads, boots, and other proper safety gear.
- wear a long-sleeved shirt, gloves, and long pants to be protected from head to toe.
- be careful in bad weather, including wet, windy, or icy conditions.
- check their bike before and after each ride.
- do other forms of exercise, such as running and weight lifting, to remain fit enough to control their bike.

For More Information

BOOKS

Kaiser, Brianna. *Look Inside a Dirt Bike*. Lerner Publications, 2024.

Stevenson, Paul. *Motocross*. Hungry Tomato, 2024.

Vonder Brink, Tracy. *Motocross*. Pogo Books, 2025.

WEBSITES

Motocross

https://americanmotorcyclist.com/Racing/motocross/

Read more about the many different types of motocross races.

Transworld Motocross

https://motocross.com/

Check out the latest news, photos, and videos at Transworld Motocross, a magazine that covers motocross and motocross racing.

Publisher's note to educators and parents: Our editors have carefully reviewed these websites to ensure that they are suitable for students. Many websites change frequently, however, and we cannot guarantee that a site's future contents will continue to meet our high standards of quality and educational value. Be advised that students should be closely supervised whenever they access the Internet.

Glossary

amateur: someone who does something without pay

arena: a place where a sporting event takes place

endurance: the ability to do something hard for a long time

event: a happening

lapping: when the leader of the race is one or more whole laps ahead of another competitor

modify: make changes

obstacle: something that blocks a path

penalize: to punish

professional: earning money from an activity that many people do for fun

Index

arena 22

boots 15, 30

dirt bike 4, 6, 12, 28

dirt track 6, 8

Dye, Edison 11

enduro 24, 25

flags 17

freestyle motocross 26

helmet 15, 30

knee pads 15, 30

motorcycle scrambling 8, 10

rules 20

supercross 22, 23

X Games 26